21st Century
Junior Library

INFOGRAPHICS: ANGLES OF ACHIEVEMENT

Sports-Graphics Jr.

Kristy Stark

Published in the United States of America by:

CHERRY LAKE PRESS
2395 South Huron Parkway, Suite 200, Ann Arbor, Michigan 48104
www.cherrylakepress.com

Reading Adviser: Beth Walker Gambro, MS Ed., Reading Consultant, Yorkville, IL

Photo Credits: © Boblgum/Getty Images, © kapona/Shutterstock, © Parinya Panyana/Shuttersock, ©fitie/Getty Images, © kbstocks/Getty Images, © Olga Streinikova/Getty Images, cover; © Jessica Orozco, 5; © Roi and Roi/Getty Images, © ONYXprj/Getty Images, 7; © nuiiun/Getty Images, © bortonia/Getty Images, © bortonia/Getty Images, © bortonia/Getty Images, 8; © photosynthesis/Getty Images, 9; © Jessica Orozco, 10; © Jessica Orozco, 11; © Jessica Orozco, 12; © GoodStudio/Shutterstock, 14; © aleksandr-mansurov-ru/Getty Images, 15; © Jessica Orozco, 17; © Yuliyan Velchev/Shutterstock, © Creativika Graphics/Shutterstock, 18; © Yuliyan Velchev/Shutterstock, 19

Cherry Lake Press is an imprint of Cherry Lake Publishing Group.

Library of Congress Cataloging-in-Publication Data has been filed and is available at catalog.loc.gov.

Cherry Lake Publishing Group would like to acknowledge the work of the Partnership for 21st Century Learning, a Network of Battelle for Kids. Please visit Battelle for Kids online for more information.

Printed in the United States of America

Note from publisher: Websites change regularly, and their future contents are outside of our control. Supervise children when conducting any recommended online searches for extended learning opportunities.

ABOUT THE AUTHOR

Kristy Stark writes books about a variety of topics, from sports to biographies to science topics. When she is not busy writing, she enjoys reading, camping, lounging at the beach, and doing just about anything outdoors. Most of all, she loves to spend time with her husband, daughter, son, and two lazy cats at their home in Southern California.

CONTENTS

ANGLES AND ARCS IN SPORTS

Angles and arcs are all around us. It is easy to find angles and arcs. They are in cars, books, and buildings. But did you know that angles and arcs can be found in sports, too?

So what are angles and arcs? Angles are formed where two lines meet. Arcs are curved lines. These curves form a part of a circle.

ANGLES AND ARCS ALL AROUND

Bodies in motion often form different types of angles.

A ball in motion creates an arc.

STATIC ANGLES AND ACTIVE ARCS

Sometimes, two lines or surfaces meet. The space they meet is called an angle. Some angles change as an athlete moves or performs. Think about the angles of an athlete's legs. The angles change as they move. Other angles are **static.** This means that they do not change as the sport is played. Think of the angles formed by the lines on a balance beam. The lines do not move or change during the gymnastics routine. So the angles are static.

STATIC VERSUS DYNAMIC ANGLES

Static

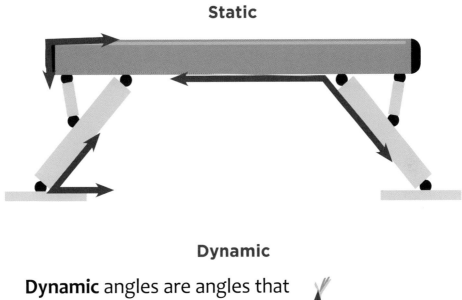

Dynamic

Dynamic angles are angles that change as an athlete moves or performs.

RIGHT ANGLES

Right angles form where two lines meet at 90°. A square has four right angles, one in each corner.

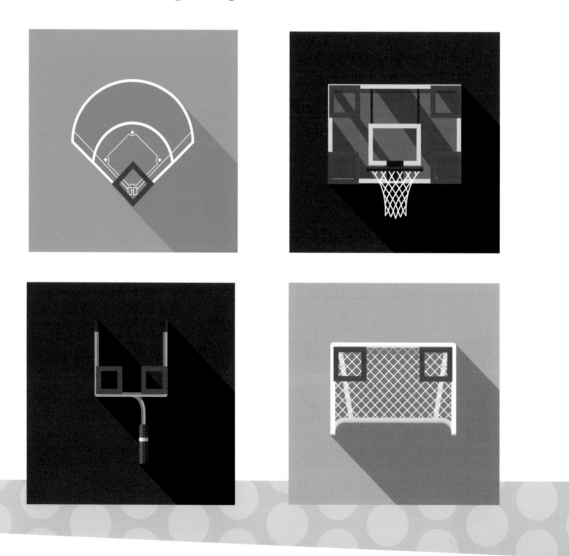

ACUTE ANGLES

Acute angles measure less than 90°. Acute means "sharp." These angles get their name because they form sharp points where the lines meet.

OBTUSE ANGLES

Obtuse angles measure more than 90°. But they are less than 180°. 180° is a straight line.

HIGH AND LOW ARCS

Imagine a quarterback's arm as he throws the ball. His arm follows an arc. The ball follows an arc, too. Long, deep passes have high arcs. Short, close passes have low arcs.

Deep Passes Make High Arcs

One deep pass is the Hail Mary. To make a Hail Mary, players take a step back and then forward to give the throw more speed. They throw the ball over their head and release it early to create a high arc.

Short Passes Make Low Arcs

A bullet pass is a short pass. Players snap their arm forward quickly. They throw the ball next to their head and release it late to create a low arc. A bullet pass is fast and short-range.

ACTIVE ARCS

Athletes often move their bodies
in arcs, not straight lines. Think of a
dancer as she leaps in the air. Her body
follows an arc. Her arms and legs form
arcs, too.

ANGLES TO ACHIEVE AN EDGE

Angles are important for athletes. In fact, angles are so important that Major League Baseball (MLB) tracks stats about them. It tracks the launch angle for different types of hits. The **launch angle** is the **vertical** angle at which the ball leaves the bat.

- Ground ball: less than 10°
- Line drive: 10° to 25°
- Fly ball: 25° to 50°
- Pop-up: greater than 50°

LAUNCH ANGLES

2022, MLB Glossary; 2021, V1 Sports Blog

Pitchers want to control batters' launch angles. They do this with pitch height. That is the distance from the ground where they release the ball. They can use it to adjust where the ball will go in the **strike zone.**

APPROXIMATE LAUNCH ANGLE BY PITCH HEIGHT

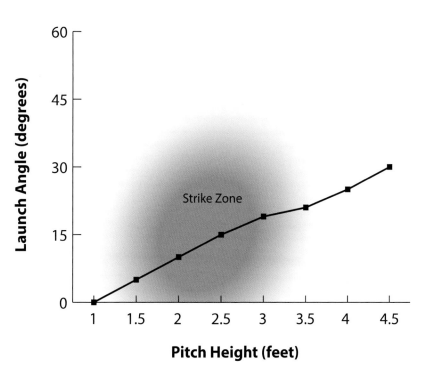

BREAKING RECORDS

An athlete's **technique** and speed are important. These features help them perform their best. The first few fractions of a second can make or break an athlete's chances of winning.

For **sprinters,** a good start is key. They need to respond quickly to the starting gun. They need to get out of the starting blocks first. A good angle can help a sprinter accelerate.

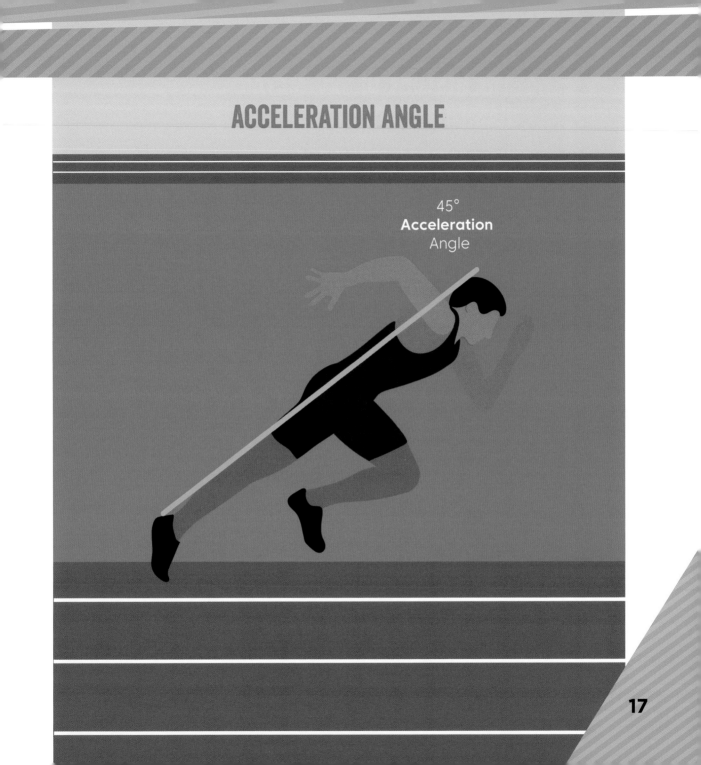

THE HISTORY OF 100-METER DASH TIMES (WOMEN)

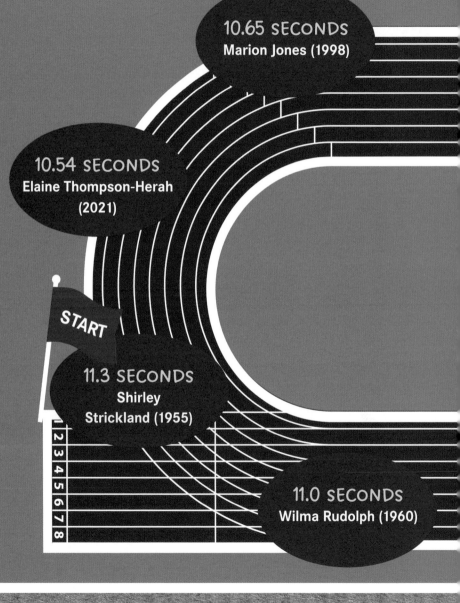

10.65 SECONDS
Marion Jones (1998)

10.54 SECONDS
Elaine Thompson-Herah (2021)

START

11.3 SECONDS
Shirley Strickland (1955)

11.0 SECONDS
Wilma Rudolph (1960)

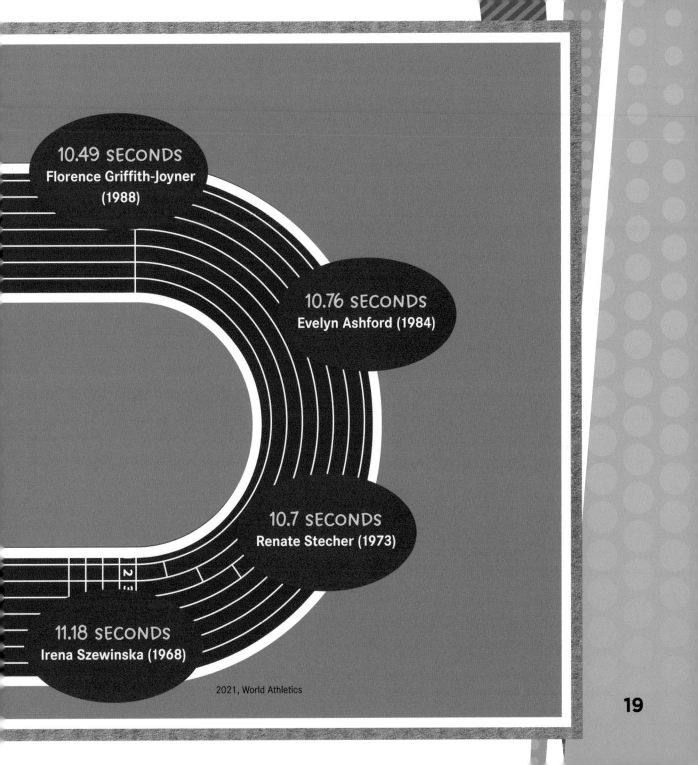

10.49 SECONDS
Florence Griffith-Joyner (1988)

10.76 SECONDS
Evelyn Ashford (1984)

10.7 SECONDS
Renate Stecher (1973)

11.18 SECONDS
Irena Szewinska (1968)

2021, World Athletics

MEN'S RUNNING WORLD RECORDS BY ATHLETE'S COUNTRY

Belgium: Bashir Abdi; 20,000 meters; 56:20:02

Morocco: Hicham El Guerrouj 1 mile; 3:43:13

Jamaica: Usain Bolt 100 meters; 9.58

Russia: Wayde Van Niekerk
400 meters; 43.03

Uganda: Joshua Cheptegei
5,000 meters; 12:35:36

Kenya: David Rudisha
800 meters; 1:40:91

Kenya: Noah Ngeny
1,000 meters; 2:11:96

2021, World Athletics

ACTIVITY

Angle Adventure

Now you know all about angles in sports. It's time to measure angles on some of your favorite players or athletes. Picture the way these athletes move their bodies. Imagine all those angles!

Materials Needed

- Magazines or computer and printer
- Paper or poster board
- Writing utensil and highlighter
- Scissors and glue
- **Protractor**

1. Find images of three to five athletes in magazines or on websites. Print or cut out the images. Glue them onto chart paper or poster board.

2. Highlight one angle on the athlete's body. Use a protractor to measure that angle.

3. Label each highlighted angle with the measurement.

Want to measure more angles? Move your body into different angles. Have a family member or friend take a picture of you in each position. Then print the pictures and glue them to paper. Repeat the steps above to measure your angles.

FIND OUT MORE

Books

Buckley, James Jr. *It's a Numbers Game! Soccer: The Math Behind the Perfect Goal, the Game-Winning Save, and So Much More!* Washington, DC: National Geographic Kids, 2020.

Ventura, Marne. *Learning STEM from Baseball.* New York: Sky Pony, 2020.

Wall, Julie. *Basketball Angles.* Huntington Beach, CA: Teacher Created Materials, 2009.

Online Resources to Explore with an Adult

Our Family Code: Measure Athlete Angles in Olympic Sports

PBS Kids: The Science of Angles: Learn Through Sports

Bibliography

Math Is Fun. Names of Angles. September 22, 2001.

Measurement of Angles. Encyclopedia.com.

MLB Glossary. February 4, 2020.

World Athletics. Records by Event. February 2021.

GLOSSARY

acceleration (ak-sell-uh-RAY-shun) the act of moving faster

acute angles (uh-KYOOT ANG-uhls) angles that measure less than 90°

dynamic (die-NA-mik) constantly active or changing

launch angle (LAWNCH ANG-uhl) the vertical angle at which a ball leaves a player's bat after being struck

obtuse angles (OB-toos ANG-uhls) angles that measure more than 90° but less than 180°

protractor (proh-TRAK-tur) a tool used to measure angles

right angles (RITE ANG-uhls) angles that measure 90°

sprinters (SPRIN-turs) runners who race over a short distance at a very fast speed

static (STAT-ik) showing little or no change or action

strike zone (STRYKE ZOHN) the area over home plate from the midpoint between a batter's shoulders and the top of the uniform pants

technique (tek-NEEK) a way of doing something that uses special knowledge or skill

vertical (VER-tuh-kuhl) positioned up and down; going straight up

INDEX